Bill Gates

By JoAnn Grote

 Wright Group

The McGraw·Hill Companies

www.WrightGroup.com

 **Wright Group**

Contents

Historical Time Line

The world has changed dramatically since Bill Gates was born. Computers and Bill's contribution to technology led to some of the changes. But there have been major changes in other areas, too. Space explorations have increased our knowledge of the universe. Satellites make it possible to view news across the world almost immediately. Advances in biological research, such as DNA, raise hopes of eliminating devastating diseases. Below is a time line of significant events in Bill Gates's life and other significant events which happened at the same time.

E-mail is introduced.

On October 28, Bill Gates is born.

Bill Gates enters Lakeside School, where he is introduced to computers.

Gates writes a program for Altair.

1955　　　　　**1968**　　　　　**1972**　　　　**1975**

　　　1964　　　　　　**1969**　　　　　　**1973**　　　　**1980**

Bill Gates enrolls at Harvard University.

The Beatles first hit the charts.

Neil Armstrong is the first human to walk on the moon.

Microsoft writes MS-DOS for IBM.

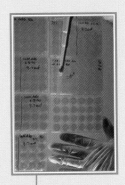

The World Wide Web is developed.

The first human receives gene therapy.

A human genome (complete set of genetic information) is first drafted.

Prince Charles and Lady Diana marry.

Microsoft introduces Windows.

1981

1982

1985

1986

1990

1994

2000

2001

Bill Gates becomes a billionaire at the age of 31.

Bill Gates marries Melinda French.

Microsoft wins antitrust lawsuit.

The first compact disc is created.

Author's Note

There are many people who have made a difference in the world—people who have changed lives in revolutionary ways. Bill Gates is one of those people. He started making a difference while he was still in high school.

Bill Gates changed the world by doing what he found most exciting: finding ways to make computers do complex and fun things. If you have ever used a computer, you have probably used a program Bill helped create.

I admire Bill Gates because he had the courage to explore the things that excited him. Then, he used what he loved to make life better for billions of people. He has changed the world forever.

As you read, see whether you think Bill Gates is a truly amazing American.

JoAnn Grote

CHAPTER ONE

READY!

Paul Allen rushed into Bill Gates's Harvard dorm room waving a copy of *Popular Electronics*. "Look, it's going to happen! And we're going to miss it!" Paul said. Bill looked at the magazine's cover. There was a picture of a box with switches on the front—the Altair computer. "World's first minicomputer kit to rival professional models," the magazine boasted.

Bill and Paul had known one day someone would make a computer small enough to fit on a desk that was inexpensive enough for the average person to afford. That day was finally here! But the Altair needed **software**. Bill and Paul decided to be the ones to write it.

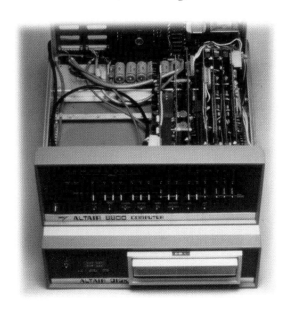

Bill Gates and Paul Allen wrote a program for the Altair computer.

Bill and Paul made an appointment to demonstrate their **program** with MITS, the company in Albuquerque, New Mexico that made the Altair. They didn't tell the company that Bill hadn't started writing the program yet. He didn't have an Altair to practice on. Paul found a book on the Altair. Then he wrote a program to make Harvard's large PDP-10 computer work like the Altair. Bill would practice his program on that computer.

Bill and Paul only had a few weeks. They worked night and day. Sometimes, they would fall asleep working. Finally, it was time for Paul to fly to Albuquerque for the demonstration.

Bill waited anxiously at Harvard. So many things could go wrong! He and Paul had still never seen an Altair. If Paul hadn't made the PDP-10 work exactly like the Altair, Bill's program wouldn't work. And what if Bill's program had a bug?

In Their Own Words

"To win big, you sometimes have to take big risks."

~Bill Gates, 1999

The phone rang. Bill answered. He was excited, yet scared. Paul told Bill how he had loaded the Altair with information it would need to read Bill's program. He described how nervous he was as he waited for the machine's screen to display the word

Bill Gates shares his love of computers with young people in Malaysia

"ready"—the signal that the Altair was ready to run Bill's program.

Bill listened as Paul described how he demonstrated the program Bill wrote. It worked perfectly, and MITS wanted to buy it!

Joy flooded over Bill as he listened to Paul's story. All their hard work had paid off! This was the beginning of a computer revolution. With the Altair using Bill's program, computers would be able to do all kinds of complicated tasks. But Bill couldn't have imagined the huge impact he would have on the world in the years ahead.

Bill Gates's early interest in computers would one day lead him to start Microsoft.

★ ★ ★ ★

How do you think computer software has changed since Bill's first program for the Altair?

Leap Back in Time

There have been many changes in tools and technology during Bill Gates's lifetime and he has contributed to many of them. When Bill was young, computers were often large enough to fill an entire room. Today, large amounts of information can be stored on a chip smaller than a thumbnail. Instead of buying a record at a record store as people did 30 years ago, we can now purchase music directly from the Internet and store it on CDs, computers, and listening devices. Check out a few of the items on these pages to see just how far tools and technology have come since Bill Gates was a child.

MICR

1980s COMPUTER

VIDEO CAMERA

VCR

LAPTOP
COMPUTER

PDA

HIP

FLOPPY
DISK

CDs

~ 11

CHAPTER TWO

Teenage Businessman

illiam Henry Gates III was born in Seattle, Washington on October 28, 1955. His father, William Henry Gates Jr., was a lawyer. His mother, Mary, was a schoolteacher and chairperson of United Way International. Both of his parents were active in charitable causes. In dinnertime conversations, William and Mary would often tell their children about the work they did.

Bill was the second of three children, and the only son. "It was a rich environment in which to live," Bill Gates later said about his family.

Growing up, Bill spent a lot of time in his basement bedroom reading and thinking. Once, when his mother called him for dinner and he didn't respond, she asked Bill what he was doing.

"I'm thinking!" he shouted back at her.

"You're thinking?"

"Yes, Mom, I'm thinking. Have you ever tried thinking?"

Mr. and Mrs. Gates decided their young son needed counseling. They thought a therapist would help Bill overcome his shyness and learn to be more obedient to his parents. After a year, the therapist told Bill's parents that his stubbornness was there to stay.

Bill Gates became interested in computer programming when he was a student at Lakeside School.

In 1968, when Bill was in eighth grade, he enrolled at Seattle's prestigious Lakeside School. His former school wasn't much of a challenge for him, and his parents hoped Lakeside would give him the stimulation he needed. That year, the students at Lakeside learned about computers.

Bill Gates's father, Bill Gates Jr.

Computers were still new, expensive, and huge! A single computer took up an entire room. Only a few large businesses and universities owned them. Lakeside School couldn't afford a computer, so the school raised money to buy time on a computer owned by General Electric. School **administrators** were certain they'd purchased enough computer time to last a whole school year, but they hadn't counted on Bill Gates and his friend, Paul Allen.

Did You Know... Bill was an Eagle Scout, and served in 1972 as a congressional intern.

The computer fascinated Bill and Paul. They wanted to spend all their time learning how it worked and how to make it perform different tasks. They skipped classes, turned homework in late, and snuck into

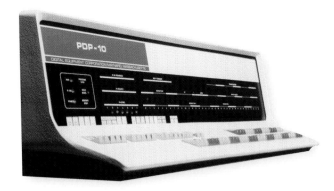

Bill Gates and Paul Allen practiced programming on a PDP-10 computer that was similar to this one.

school at night to spend more time on the computer. They used up all the school's computer time in just a few weeks.

While they both loved computers, different things about the machines interested them. Paul's interest was working with operating systems. Operating systems make it possible for a computer to run programs. Bill's passion was creating computer programs. One of the first programs Bill wrote was for a tick-tack-toe game. They programmed the computer so it would try thousands of different tick-tack-toe moves.

In Their Own Words

"The teachers thought we were quite unusual."

~Bill Gates on his teachers' reactions to him and his computer-obsessed friends

Lakeside began renting computer time from a company called Computer Center Corporation, or CCC. Bill, Paul, and some of their friends found ways through the computer's security system. They changed files on the computer and caused the computer to crash a number of times.

The people at CCC weren't pleased that Bill and his friends had **hacked** into their system, but they were impressed. They hired Bill, Paul, and their friends, Rick Weiland and Kent Evans, to test the system and find more problems. Once the bugs were identified, CCC's engineers could fix them, or at least warn clients about them. The boys formed a company called the Lakeside Programming Group and went to work for CCC. At age 13, Bill was a businessman.

Every night, the Lakeside Programming Group rode their bikes to CCC after everyone else was gone. They found hundreds of bugs for the company, while learning more and more about computers and programs. Bill learned a little more than the people at CCC would have liked.

Early in their careers, Bill Gates and Paul Allen rode their bicycles to work.

Every CCC computer user had a password. Bill got past the passwords and into files he wasn't supposed to see. He was very excited to be doing something so sneaky. Then the computer crashed, and Bill was caught. He and his friends weren't allowed to work at CCC any longer.

Lakeside Programming Group joined another company and began to create a payroll program. After a heated argument, Paul put

Bill Gates (right) and Paul Allen (left) continued working together until Allen left the company in 1983 to battle Hodgkin's disease. He founded Vulcan Inc. in Seattle, where he now serves as chairman.

himself in charge of Lakeside Programming Group and kicked Bill out. He soon realized, however, that the payroll program could not be completed without Bill's help. "If you want me to come back," Bill said, "you have to let me be in charge. But this is a dangerous thing, because if you put me in charge this time, I'm going to want to be in charge forever." Paul had no choice but to ask Bill to come back.

Before payroll programs were created, one of the best ways to keep track of employee hours was through a time clock.

In high school, Bill Gates and Paul Allen started a company called Traf-O-Data that measured traffic flow in Seattle.

Bill continued to spend more and more time working with computers and less and less time in class. He read ahead in his math book so he could skip class and still pass. One year, he challenged himself to get straight A's without ever taking a book home. He succeeded, and even placed among the ten highest scorers on a national math test.

By tenth grade, Bill was teaching others how to use computers. He was also writing computer programs for the school, including a scheduling program that made Bill and Paul the only boys in classes filled with the prettiest girls in school.

Did You Know... Bill was awkward around girls. It took Bill two weeks to work up the courage to ask a girl to the prom. She turned him down.

Bill Gates originally enrolled at Harvard University to study law.

Bill graduated from Lakeside and, in 1973, enrolled at Harvard University. He decided to study law, like his father, but computers were far more interesting. Sometimes, he would stay up all night working on Harvard's computers and fall asleep in class during the day. Other times, it was an all-night card game that made him doze off in class.

Bill Gates's father, William Gates Jr.

After Bill created the computer language for the Altair, he gave up on law. He left Harvard in his junior year and moved to Albuquerque, New Mexico to begin his next adventure—Microsoft.

★ ★ ★ ★

Bill's parents were concerned he wasn't making a wise decision when he quit Harvard to build Microsoft. How do you think the world of computers would be different today if Bill had stayed at Harvard instead?

CHAPTER THREE

Microsoft

Bill and Paul were convinced that when people saw everything the Altair could do with Bill's software, other companies would start making **microcomputers**. The microcomputers would all need software, and Bill and Paul wanted to be the ones to provide it.

In July of 1975, Bill and Paul started a software company they called Micro-Soft, short for microcomputer software. Eventually, the hyphen was dropped and the company became Microsoft. Microsoft was the first company whose purpose was to create software.

Some of the first people Bill and Paul hired to help with Microsoft were former classmates from Lakeside School. They worked hard, but wore gym shoes and jeans to work.

Bill (far right) with Microsoft executives in 1983.

In 1979, Microsoft moved to Bill's hometown of Seattle. Bill had missed being near lakes or the ocean when he lived in New Mexico. He bought an expensive home with an indoor swimming pool beside Lake Washington.

The next year, International Business Machines (IBM) asked Microsoft to develop an operating system for IBM's first PC, or personal computer. IBM was the largest computer manufacturer in the world.

Bill Gates moved Microsoft to Seattle in 1979. The company is still located in the Seattle area.

Microsoft didn't have time to develop an operating system for IBM from scratch. So Bill bought a system called QDOS (Quick and Dirty Operating System) and changed it to work for IBM's PC. He called the new program MS-DOS (Microsoft Dirty Operating System).

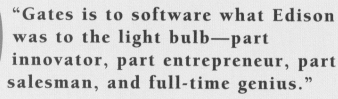

In Their Own Words

"Gates is to software what Edison was to the light bulb—part innovator, part entrepreneur, part salesman, and full-time genius."

~People *magazine, Dec 26, 1983*

Microsoft products are used in offices and homes all over the world.

IBM's PC came out in 1981, and instantly became the computer of choice in the business world. "Microsoft was founded based on my vision of a personal computer on every desk and in every home," Bill said. And he wanted them all to use Microsoft software! By the end of 1983, almost all PCs used MS-DOS. This meant millions of dollars to Microsoft.

It also meant Bill could now spend time working on new **applications**. First, Microsoft did some research, asking people what they wanted their computers to do. Then, Bill and his employees developed software to meet people's needs. Today, two of their most popular software programs are Excel for making spreadsheets and Microsoft Word for written projects.

This 1981 IBM PC (right) used Microsoft software.

Over the next several years, Bill continued to hire the best and smartest people he could find, often hiring people based on their IQ level. Many were right out of college. Like Bill, they worked long hours and enjoyed their jobs. "If you don't like to work hard and be intense and do your best, this is not the place to work," Bill said.

In 1985, construction began on a new headquarters for Microsoft in Redmond, Washington, fifteen miles from Seattle. Bill wanted the almost-one-thousand employees to feel at home. Today, the Redmond campus, as the headquarters is called, has places to play, jog, or relax, in addition to work. It includes gardens, walking paths, athletic fields, basketball courts, and a lake named for Bill.

Bill dreamed of computers that were easy to use, displayed in color, and used images besides numbers, letters, and lines. There were computer systems already that could display graphics,

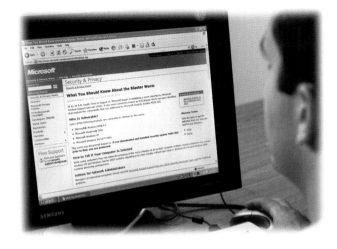

Today, Microsoft offers customers on-line support for its programs.

but they weren't easy to use. Bill wanted a graphic system that could be used with a mouse or a keyboard. Numerous documents could be displayed on it at once in different "windows" —just like numerous documents could be laid out on a desk.

Keeping It Simple

Although Bill Gates is one of the wealthiest men in the world, he doesn't often act the part. He drives his own car (and drives fast enough to get a ticket now and then), flies coach or business class (he doesn't own a plane), and has always loved fast food and all-night diners. In Seoul, Korea, his simple clothes and not-so-styled hair have made him a fashion icon. Gates appreciates his wealth, but he tries not to let it go to his head. He's raising his children to have the same values.

Bill and his coworkers spent three years creating such a system, and introduced it in 1985 as Microsoft Windows 1.03. Sales were low. The program was slow to use, and most computers didn't yet have the underlying technology to take advantage of the best features. But Bill had hopes for the future of Windows.

Bill had been right about Windows, too. By 1993, one million copies of Windows were selling a month. Two years later, an upgraded version of Windows was released. It sold seven million copies in the first six weeks.

Bill Gates takes a small break after the 1985 release of Windows.

Counterpoint

Microsoft vs.
The U.S. Government

In 1998, the U.S. Justice Department thought that Microsoft was too powerful. It ordered Microsoft to share information about its products with competitors. The company complied. Then, in 2000, the government ordered Microsoft to split into two companies: one that produced Windows and one that produced other software. Bill Gates and his lawyers fought these decisions and won the case in 2001.

As a result of Bill Gates's charitable contributions, people are able to use computers to get information.

Now that Microsoft was a huge success—and would become even more successful with the arrival of the Internet—Bill's mother thought it was time Bill gave something back. She wanted him to work with the United Way, but Bill didn't think he had the time. The technology industry was highly competitive, and Bill wanted Microsoft to stay on top. But his mother persuaded him.

Bill asked the employees of Microsoft to come together in the effort—there were even contests to see which department could raise the most money. In a short time, Microsoft raised millions of dollars for United Way. This was just the beginning.

Computer mouse

In 1993, Bill read an article about the health crisis in underprivileged countries. People were dying at alarming rates, in some cases, of illnesses that were no longer a problem in the United States. The article mentioned one virus that killed five hundred thousand children a year. Bill was stunned. If this were true, why weren't there more newspaper articles about it? Why weren't people more upset?

Bill and Melinda Gates

Bill shared the article with his **fiancée**, Melinda French. They had met at Microsoft in 1987, and Bill proposed in 1993. They were married in Hawaii on January 1, 1994. Sadly, Bill's mother died later that year.

After months of research and planning, Bill, Melinda, and Bill's father founded the William H. Gates Foundation, named after and headed by Bill Gates Sr. The foundation's goals were to close the technology gap between wealthy nations and poorer nations, to improve education, and to improve the health of people all over the world. By now, Bill was a billionaire, and through his foundation, he decided to give 95 percent of his money away.

In Their Own Words

"[If] we put our minds to it and spend the money in the right way, then we can make a dramatic difference."

~*Bill Gates*

In March of 1997, Bill visited Soweto, South Africa. The trip was supposed to be about technology, but Bill soon realized people of Soweto and poorer areas in South Africa needed medicine far more than they needed computers. That year, the William H. Gates Foundation had

Through the Bill and Melinda Gates foundation, Bill Gates works to help people around the world.

$1.6 billion to donate, making it the richest charity in the United States. Two years later, the foundation was renamed the Bill and Melinda Gates Foundation. It continues to donate money for scholarships, computers for schools and public libraries, and medical research and **vaccines**.

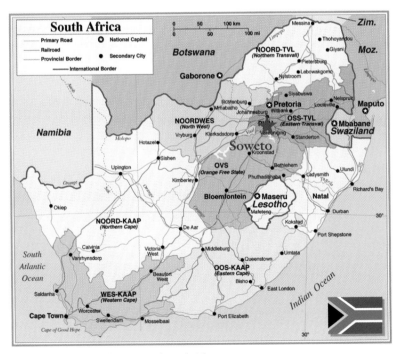

Soweto is located in the center of South Africa.

CHAPTER FOUR

The Future

Microsoft is one of the most successful companies in the history of the world. It has made Bill one of the world's wealthiest citizens. He became a billionaire at age 31.

Bill continues to work hard to keep Microsoft on top. He seems most excited about technology that will allow people to handwrite documents as a computer simultaneously types them and computers that will recognize voices. He knows the road ahead will not be entirely smooth for Microsoft, but there is a lot to be learned by making mistakes.

Today, he is more involved in creating these technologies and

less involved in running the company. He couldn't be happier. "[I have] a chance to focus on some very important work," he said in an interview, "the kind of work I enjoy most of all."

Bill Gates and Microsoft continue to develop technology designed to make tasks in everyday life easier.

Though Microsoft keeps Bill busy, he makes time for his family and other hobbies, including golf, bridge, and driving. Bill and Melinda have two daughters, Jennifer and Phoebe, and one son, Rory.

The Gates home on Lake Washington

Bill had a new home built on Lake Washington across from Seattle. High-tech products fill the house. It cost over $50 million and took many years to build.

The Gates Estate

There's no place like Bill Gates's home—yet. If all goes according to Microsoft's plan, someday you also will have a home that's run by a computer. Gates's home is partly underground and includes a trampoline room, a theater, a salmon stream, and three garages. The most remarkable thing about the house is that it has a computer brain. Visitors wear small badges that are read by the computer. The computer adjusts the light, music, temperature, and electronic wall art to meet each visitor's tastes. What happens when there's more than one person in a room? The computer is set to choose one person's preference over another, and if Bill is in the room, his preferences win.

Conclusion

Bill Gates grew up loving computers and turned that love into a multi-billion dollar business. He has created a whole new industry and jobs for Americans and people around the world. Through his work, he has made our society much more efficient. Bill Gates is an incredible businessman and innovator who has changed the face of technology and will continue to do so far into the future.

Today, many tasks can be accomplished using computers.

Bill Gates speaking about the benefits of computers

Glossary

administrators people who manage the affairs of a school, business, or government agency

applications computer programs designed for a specific task, such as word processing

fiancée a woman who is engaged to be married

hacked to have bypassed a computer's security system and accessed private information

microcomputers small computers whose "brains" are computer chips

program instructions that tell a computer what to do

software instructions that tell a computer to perform a specific application

vaccines substances, usually injected, that protect against disease

Index